A Heart Lighter
Than a Feather

Divine Ishq

Salma Yusuf

Copyright © 2022 by Salma Yusuf **First**

paperback edition October 2022 ISBN 978-1-

3999-3207-3

Dedication to God

I was looking for a home outside of me.
Till one day I found my home within.

Salma Yusuf

CONTENTS

The Poems

A Heart Lighter Than a Feather

When the heart is lighter than a feather,

It becomes like a bird, flying freely above the sky.

Dreams come true instantly;

riding on a cloud of joy.

Where no self-pity or anger resides;

Where only a world of light and love lives:

Pure heaven.

A perfume of love spreads around the world;

giggling like a child, echoing only rainbows of

innocence.

Your tread is light, as if not touching the ground,

lighter than a feather.

Only the wind of love carries you into the

heaven within yourself,

Where you can listen to the melodies within

our hearts;

To the glory that exists beyond our

perception.

The Shape of My Heart

When the shape of your heart grows bigger

than your mind,

divine love will flow through you, washing

all your fears and doubts away, filling you

with a celestial light.

We have forgotten to be intimate with our

inner ourselves;

Forgotten what we looked like before we

were born.

We fight our reflections in the mirror of life,

but end up only fighting our false identities.

We have worn different masks,

not realising our true inner being within ourselves:

Waiting to discover and

rekindled.

Lost and Found

I was like a fish living in a puddle of water

Thinking I was limited; incapable of finding

the ocean.

Lost in the shore my wrong beliefs,

blaming the world and circumstances

Till I finally, I found the real me in the midst

of me,

Hiding like the sun behind a cloud;

Full of unlimited potentialities, like an ocean

without end.

I have decided not to die before singing my

song before dancing… my dance.

Be Spontaneous

Be spontaneous,

Like a child who swings at the park with joy,
Giggle,
Remembering the promising beauty of life,

Be ridiculous and dare to cross the borders of
your limitations,
Dare to laugh in the face of what is thrown at
you,
Enjoy the fresh cotton of life;

Dance like the birds of paradise,

and celebrate your uniqueness in the jungle of life.

I am Unconquerable

Nothing can conquer me because I am a
divine being and pure spirit—free from all
illusion.

I am clad against circumstance and evils:
Like a phoenix, a challenge strengthens
me. I conquer my ego,
I mould my consciousness the way I like.

I manufacture my reality, weaving infinite
possibilities,
Dancing like Shiva—destroying limiting
beliefs and creating heaven within me.

Layer by Layer

Strip all layers of the false self.

Become no one—an empty vessel for divine
light to fill—
And your true self will emerge,

To achieve the divine, you must stop the

mind's endless chatter and all self-pursuits.

And enter deep silence and tune into your

spiritual heart.

You will hear the whispers of wisdom

and silent knowledge that lie within.

The Light of Awareness

Awareness is a light that frees us from the
conditioning of the mind.

A beam of light enters our seated dark
aspect—
like a traffic light, it controls and
organises our thoughts;

It prevents the wrong thoughts from flowing
into the road of our being,

It calms and grants pure thought to access the
surface of our minds, like a lotus flower on
muddy water;

The light allows thoughts to flow into our
being and environment, like a joyful squirrel
jumping from tree to tree with his fluffy tail.

It's like a safety bag that prevents negative
thoughts from crushing our lives.

Soul Guitar

Every soul is like a guitar, with its own unique tone.

Our mission in this life is to find the right string and tune it to its full potential.

The world will enjoy its song.

Only through experience you will find the right tune for the right string; find your soul's tone.

Then, your soul's song will inspire other souls to find their own tune and rhythm.

Inner Flower

When we envision for ourselves, our life becomes a constant celebration, bliss, and harmony.

Nothing in the world can make you happy or content until you change your inner world

Water your inner flowers in your garden

Then your flowers will blossom into fragrances with beautiful colours

Spreading your inner rainbow across your own being.

Mind Breathing

When we enter silence, the mind breathes
fresh air like lungs,

it breathes out its constant thoughts, of
heavy burden from judging, living in the
past and future.

Do we give our mind a break from its burden
of illusion? can one day we wake up with no
thoughts? can we break the chain of our
thoughts and its concern?
Do we have a comma ,,,,,,,,,,, in our
thoughts, to see the beauty and simplicity of
life.

We think our knowledge and intellect can
lead us to peace within,
we spend our life thinking we know
everything, but at the end we realise our
mind failed us in so many ways and
obscured us from perceiving life accurately.

When we stop thinking.........

suddenly we hear settle sounds of air,

surroundings, neighbours, languages we
never heard of
Eventually we can hear the settle sound of
our being,
a sound waiting to be heard, expressed, and
valued.
It contains all the answers to all our lives, the
secret of the universe

A Heart Full of Wisdom

The heart is full of wisdom: all knowing.

It connects with the universe through a web
of golden thread.
Let the mind be still; become the reflection
of your heart.
Allow the mind to become a diver. Let it
dive into the heart's ocean.

Allow it to bring knowledge and love to you.

Truth From Our Heart

Truth, beauty, and wisdom comes from
our heart

The secret lies in our heart

Open your heart, the universe within
You!

Our destiny transcribed in our heart

If we don't listen to the whisper of our
heart

We drift away from our destiny till we
become aliens to ourselves like a piece of
wood driven by a wild river of life

The Heart Doesn't Sleep

The mind and body both sleep

,But the heart does not:

It transmits subtle, intuitive information

To our being, while the material body
and mind sleep. Listen to the frequency
of the heart;
Wash and indulge in its pure aroma
that awakens the soul from its
slumber.

Life is Sexual

Life and death are sexual,

Heaven and earth are sexual,

Water and sky are sexual,

Breaths in   out are

sexual,

The conscious and subconscious minds are

sexual,

The physical and spiritual world are sexual;

The entire universe is in a sexual mood.

It's a world of conceiving, desiring, and

achieving!

Inner Intelligence

Tap into your inner Google,

where all the answers lie.

God installed in us an intelligent GPS

guidance:

Technology is just a tiny imitation of the

Google within us.

Be receptive and empty of ego, tap into your

internal apps;

Unfreeze your inner screen.

Divine GPS works on the heart at the level of

love and joy;

When it is lost, we lose our way.

Microscope

Looking at blood morphology taught me
how cells morph according to their
conditions

If they are healthy, they look in good shape
and are pleasant to look at them

I smile and congratulate them for being
healthy

I celebrate with them with my eyes filled with
gladness

when they have irregular shapes and dull
they tell the sad story of their owner

How they are trying to heal, but the patient is
not listening to their cell's advice

Weeping with irregularities

Neutrophils fighting to clear the war that
manifested in the body

Our cells morphology is just a reflection
of our internal battle within ourselves

Trees

If trees don't empty themselves of shrivelled
leaves,

How will they receive nutrients for new
leaves to grow?

It is the same question for humanity.

If we don't empty ourselves of our ego and
social conditioning,

How will we receive the glory of God?

How will our souls be filled with his
blessings and light?

Neutral World

Everything is neutral. Nothing is bad, nor
particularly good.

It's how we label things that matter:

We see the world coloured by our personal
history;

Until we clear our emotional baggage,

We won't be able to see reality,

Through a neutral lens.

God

He is my edges, my pillar and my conners

He is in my middle and around me

He is all of me

Stretched Silence

We need silence between words,

between breath.

Between blinking eyes,

Stretched Silence to reflect and bring new

ideas into our lives,

To refine and refurbish us,

Rearranging and releasing what is not

serving us.

Life Without Fear

I will ruffle my wings and fly high like a bird without looking back at my past or thinking about my future.

I will just enjoy the present moment,

and drink the nectar of life without worry or fear.

Each moment is like a heartbeat, pumping treasures of life through my body.

My best friend is my heart that beats in harmony with my breath. It promises me it will beat at this moment,

But without guarantee for the next. My heart tells me, 'Enjoy life while I am beating,

while I regulate your blood and enhance your life, allowing you to experience the richness of life'.

Perspective

The entire universe exists in your heart

The illusion lives in your mind

The heart is like an ocean with endless

possibilities

While the mind is a peddle with limited

possibilities,

The heart is like opening a door to unlimited

realities of existence

The mind is looking through keyhole, to

limited perspective

Fear blocks our internal sun

Do not allow the illusion of fear blocking

your light

Clear the mirror of your heart to reflect pure

divine love and bliss

Heart's Message

Every heart came to fulfill a message

Let the heart flows its content to enrich the
world

To bring to the world peace and love

Certificate

We live in this life believing we must gain a
certificate in something to win at
life's game.

When we live life detached from our soul's
purpose and
adopt foreign purposes,
we become like everyone else,

just a product of what society says we should
like or have...
Till we go through a crisis

that shatters our world view.
We realise the world is just a reflection of
our inner world.
We go within and realise we have so many
gifts and qualities.
We trust ourselves, using our talents.

Certificates from within are more valid than
any piece of paper.

Homeless Spiritually

If we don't connect within and find God
within

We are homeless because true home is not
somewhere outside of us

Some buildings, country we seek or after life
heaven we live

It's within us and if we don't turn within to
our true home

We become homeless through eternity

Switch Off

Switch off the outside world and tune into your inner-world:

Focusing on the outer world prevents you from seeing the pure truth—

Misleading you, like a sheep lost in a jungle, a victim of circumstances.

But focusing on your inner world will lead you to the ultimate truth and liberate you.

Illuminate the Page of Your Life

Illuminate the page of your life by paddling,

then diving, into the seas of the unknown.

Experiencing unlimited capacity.

Don't become imprisoned in a repetitive,

predictable life that only solidifies your

world view and constrains your expansion

Welcome to the unknown—take a risk,

fearless spirit like an eagle!

Grovelling

Grovelling in the muds of our senses

Losing our touch with our divine within

us Identifying false self with our real self

The mud only promises us to suffer and

humiliation into earthly materials and desires

Forgetting who we really are

Wasting our true heritage that waiting us

within to be claimed

Stirring the Self

Stirring the self is important to shake
away the dust of a static identity.

Our viewpoints need upheaval to purge
prejudice and make space for a new idea to
take over,

Like a spider who, every time his web is
destroyed, creates a new one.

Transforming our inner thoughts will
revolutionise our entire being,

Moulding our life into continuous
enjoyment—dancing flamingo-bright with
life.

Faith

Faith is an act of the heart

Doubt is the act of the mind

Bless he who has faith

To surrender to the source with ultimate faith

Smell

I smell life

I smell the green trees

Evoking all the happy emotions

I smell white roses that sleep in my heart like
snow white
Ready to be awakened

I smell the soil promising me

That my dream will grow and come true

Inner Soul Symphony

Listen to your soul's symphony—

it loves to share its glorious song with others,

It shows the way out of the darkness haunting

humanity.

For eternity, it sings like a curlew.

Your soul has the power to open wisdom's

gate;

Allow it to unfold like a blossom.

Warmth of Heart

When we tune in to warmth of our heart

It rescues us and shelter us from the wimp of
our mind

It safeguards us from our mind
programming, from outside ourselves

Our heart radiates the love and harmony like a
twitter bird

Spreading its song across the garden
singing confidently with its own
uniqueness

When Night Falls Upon Us

Every night, when the mind lulls to sleep, the

soul tiptoes, escaping mind's constraints.

Travelling through the multiverse to explore,

with curiosity;

Expanding its awareness.

And breaking free from daily life's limited

awareness.

Flow

Life is in constant flow, like a dancing firefly,
weaving

an ocean of light into the fabric of our reality.
Within our bodies, blood circulates,
Air flows through our respiratory system;
Air and water collaborate.
These are our body's teachers,
guide us with life's wisdom.

They are teaching us unity

To live in harmony with everything in life

To celebrate our differences, it doesn't
matter if the cell is a liver, kidney or a heart
They all, at the end, one unit

As humanity, we are one unit like cells

Attachment

Attachment destroys our freedom to explore;

It constricts our thoughts and limits our
options.
Attachment is a disease of the mind,
condemning the soul to slavery.

The cure ? Detachment. Becoming an
observer of ourselves;
 To see the game of our mind purely.

Life's road is not always straight—

it has roundabouts, junctions, and corners.

Stuck, we repeat the same cycle again and
again.
We can only experience the fullness of life if
we decide to take a winding road into the
unknown.

Tried it My Own Way

I have tried it in my own way; it didn't work
out perfectly.

Then I surrendered to my God within me,
and my faith worked like a magician.
 I realised that human nature, without
God/faith, is limited and baseless.

 The God within us holds an infinite magic.

Following God's path, you swim in an ocean
of love and peace beyond intellect; beyond
ego.
Because God's way is inconceivable and
incomprehensible,
All we can do is surrender to his will and
love.

Dream of Reality

Reality is a dream which changes its seasons.

Now we are in the season of summer, my
dreams taste fruity;

It feels like a palm tree is brushing over my
throat, squeezing all the oxygen out of my
lungs and replacing it with pure, luscious
love;

Summer heat feels like I'm bending into an
easy downward dog, chanting 'OM';

Or like a twinkling star that shines through
millions of rays of light,

Filling my heart with the warmth of a summer
breeze and the humidity of sensual love.

Belonging

The mind belongs to the heart

Our life instruction sealed within the treasury
of our heart

Coherence between mind and heart must be to
function

In harmony within ourselves
and with the world

The Self

Does self-attack the self

We all like oneself-one entity

When we fight our own self

We become like an autoimmune disease

Attacking its own self

Afflicting all other cells

And causing permanent suffering and harm

As humanity, we are like that

We become an autoimmune disease,

attacking oneself our brothers and sisters

Not realising we are one!

Whale's Belly

When we refuse the divine calling,

We get stuck in the dark world's

belly.

Like Jonah, stuck within the darkness of a

whale,

In this dark world, we become the victim of

our own self-imposed limitations

Till we learn the lesson:

Then the whale will spit us onto the shore of

our divine self.

Rise above the dark world, raise your

consciousness and see the beam of light

through the blowhole of this whale.

Home

I came here into this world seeking a home

Looking for a face that I know

Moving from home to home

From country to a country

From work, to work

Till I found out the home and destination are

within me

Calling me softly and gently to seek that

glowing internal blessing of home

 A home sweater and wormer than a honey

The home was my divine self

My true self that was telling me all the time

These masks am carrying all the time are not

my true self or home

it lies within my heart, glowing like a sun

shining a beam of light within,

The entire earth and universe are within me

Everyone and everything became my home

Because I have found my inner home

The divine home within

The Path

This path of life is not an outward

Is an inward path

Where we reach our core of our being

Waiting to be discovered

Layer by

layers Like an

onion

Peeling ourselves from our own delusion

News of The Heart

I don't trust the news of my mind

But I trust the news of my heart

I feel a warm liquid love poured into the

landscape of my being

That makes every cell of my being

reverberate

And celebrate with glory and love

Another level of liveness opens up into my

inner awareness

Freeing me from my mind's illusions and

flittering

Ice & Water

Nature teaches us how our life should be

And how to become fluid in this life

In tune with anything that is

Practicing union and harmony with life

rhythm

The water can evaporate and become a cloud

in the sky   .

We also have 70% water and we can

transcend our physicality and transform

ourselves into heights above the mountain

Rain our potential and radiate our inner light

out to the world

Or we become a boiling water boiled with our

emotions and challenges

But know boiling us in this life

Is what makes us transform from our

previous state into different state

And transcend those challenges which
made us lose our way into an alchemy for
philosopher stone

But where we freeze our potential and our
life into one state and identity with it

We become stagnant and we lose the
meaning of our life, stuck with lower self

Let's melt our ego into vapour of love nectar

The Whisper of Your Being

Listen to the whisper of your being:

You will feel a sensation prickling in your
bones,

Waves of vibrations moves across my skin
from head to toe, an ecstatic sensation, like a
well, echoing a forgotten truth.

A seed of acorn waiting to be nourished,
watered, and grow a giant oak tree.

Steering Away

Steering away from your mind's inner chatter

Is like sitting in a fluffy cloud buffeted by
the wind's changes

Leaving you in a turmoil of inconsistency.

To ride a cloud in a different direction
To steer away from mind's dictation
You must rise above the clouds
Into the permanent sky, without limits.

diving into an infinite sea of wisdom and
potential,

where permanent inner peace and smiles lie,

undisturbed by any waves of negative
thought.

Aligned With Your Heart

When we align with our heart,

Everything falls into place.

We become more youthful, radiant and

prosperous

We struggle in life when we choose to follow

the path of limited self-belief—

Then suffering starts. Although we have

everything, heaviness in our body and

clutters in our mind creeps and tiptoes in…

Then our life becomes unfulfilled. A rush of

emptiness invades our being:

Our heart is telling us something. Life slaps

us in every direction

Until one day, we stop resisting and start

following the North Star of our heart without

understanding why.

The mind won't comprehend the reality of

the heart.

But when the mind quietens, it swims in the
ocean of the heart like a playful a seal,
squeaking with joy, clapping its flippers
together.

About the Author

Salma Yusuf is a poet who is used to looking at life through a different lens, literally. Her studies in science morphology mean she's been looking at cells under a microscope for a long time. Looking at life on a deeper level and finding connection finding connections between science, nature and faith prompted her to look inward with the same perspective. Once she viewed herself in a new light, taking up meditation and yoga, her inner light shone brighter than ever, and she could finally see it. Her poetry brings words to the light in all of us and speaks to the human spirit, our grit and determination, our unwillingness to give up, and everything that makes us perfectly imperfect.

Salma currently lives in Manchester, UK. As a woman from an African background, she's faced many struggles throughout her life, but none she couldn't overcome. She's still fighting, proving that she's limitless in every aspect of her life. She hopes to help others wake their divinity and love within themselves. After all, she knows that life is a journey, and our inner light can guide us through the darkest moments.